100 Words to Learn in Spanish
Children's Learn Spanish Books

Copyright 2016

All Rights reserved. No part of this book may be reproduced or used in any way or form or by any means whether electronic or mechanical, this means that you cannot record or photocopy any material ideas or tips that are provided in this book

Hola!
Do you wanna know some Spanish words?

Read on and learn 100 Spanish words.

a
to, at

ahora
now

alguno
some; someone

año
year

así
like that

bien
well

cada
each, every

como
like, as

con
with

cosa
thing

creer
to believe

cuando
when

dar
to give

de
of, from

deber
should, ought to

decir
to tell, say

dejar
to let, leave

desde
from, since

después
after

día
day

donde
where

dos
two

él
he

el / la
the

ella
she

ellas
them

en
in, on

encontrar
to find

entonces
so, then

entre
between

ese
that (m)

esa
that (f)

eso
that

estar
to be

este
this (m)

esta
this (f)

grande
large, great, big

haber
to have

hablar
to speak, talk

hacer
to do, make

hasta
until, up to; even

hombre
man, husband

ir
to go

llegar
to arrive

llevar
to take, carry

lo
the (+ noun)

más
more

me
me

menos
less, fewer

mi
my

mismo
same

mucho
much, many, a lot

muy
very, really

nada
nothing

ni
not even, neither, nor

nuevo
new

o
or

otro
other, another

para
for, to, in order to

parecer
to seem, look like

parte
part, portion

pasar
to pass, spend (time)

pero
but, yet, except

poco
little few; a little bit

poder
to be able to, can

poner
to put (on); get (+ adj.)

por
by, for, through

porque
because

primero
first

que
that, which

qué
what?, which?, how

quedar
to remain, stay

querer
to want, love

saber
to know

se
-self, oneself

seguir
to follow

ser
to be

sí
yes

si
if, whether

siempre
always

sin
without

sobre
on top of, over, about

su
his, her, their, your

también
also

tan
such, a, too, so

tanto
much

tener
to have

tiempo
time, weather

todo
all, every

un
a, an

uno
one

ver
to see

vez
time, occurrence

vida
life

y
and

ya
already, still

yo
I

Common Spanish Phrases

Buenos días.
booEHN-os DEE-as
Good morning.

Buenas tardes.
booEHN-as TAR-dehs
Good afternoon.

Buenas noches.
booEHN-as NO-chehs
Good evening.

Estoy bien.
ehs-TOY bee-EHN
I am fine.

Mucho gusto.
MOO-choh GOOS-toh
Nice to meet you.

¿Te divertiste?
Did you have fun?

Share this book to your friends!

www.ingramcontent.com/pod-product-compliance
Lightning Source LLC
LaVergne TN
LVHW061320060426
835507LV00019B/2247